Behind the Scenes

by Robert R. O'Brien
illustrated by Beth Buffington

MODERN CURRICULUM PRESS

Pearson Learning Group

It starts with a vision. A film director gets an idea of how a film should look. Maybe the script calls for a small spaceship to fly the hero of the film to another world. Maybe the script calls for a talking animal. Maybe the script calls for the action to take place in a far-off location, in the midst of a tornado, or in a sinking ship.

We have all seen these scenes in some of our favorite movies. The scenes have awed us, scared us, thrilled us, or made us laugh because they look realistic. Special effects allow the filmmaker to deceive the viewer.

Sometimes this is the result of computer animation. Sometimes it is the result of clever model making. Sometimes it is just a simple trick of fooling the eye. Sometimes it is a combination of many techniques. But movie making is a constant search for ways to use science to create illusions.

Let's look at how it got started. Then we'll find out how these scenes are created.

Before movies were invented, performers would entertain people by using science. They would make people think they were seeing something that wasn't really there. For instance, a performer would make someone seem to disappear from inside a box. In reality, the person inside the box was holding a mirror. That mirror would reflect a false panel. The viewer would see the reflection of the false panel. This would make it look as if the box were empty.

The first special effects people in the film industry were these same performers. They already knew how to use science to entertain. But people weren't coming to watch them anymore. They were more interested in movies. So the performers began to perform behind the scenes in movies.

It's hard to think of a time without movies. Yet moving pictures were once a new invention. People watching a film for the first time had strong reactions because the films seemed very realistic. The effect was very powerful, and sometimes scary. A film of a train pulling into a station caused some people to run from the theater screaming. They thought the train was going to run them down! Another early film shows a man pointing a gun at the camera. To the viewer it looked as if the gun were pointed right at him or her. The first time it was shown, some members of the audience fainted. They thought they were going to be shot!

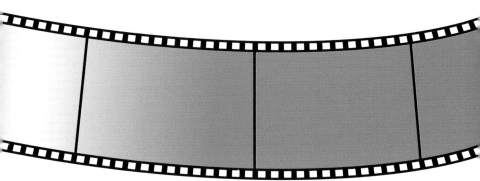

After a while, people got used to seeing the movies. As people became used to the idea of seeing "moving pictures" of ordinary things, they wanted to see something new. The filmmakers wanted to give audiences more thrills. More special effects were invented and used. Amazingly, some of the earliest techniques are still in use today.

One of the first special effects was the use of miniatures. Albert E. Smith and J. Stuart Blackton created the first "news" film by staging a miniature sea battle. In 1899, the American Navy had won a battle against the Spanish fleet in Manila Bay. The two men had read the news of the victory from a telegraph.

They cut out photographs of ships and put them on sticks. They used them like puppets and filmed them in a small tank full of water. They rigged up little explosions and fires and filmed the ships maneuvering through clouds of smoke. Though it was only two minutes long, it was an instant hit.

Miniatures are used whenever it is too expensive to shoot *on location.* "On location" means filming in the actual place where the story is supposed to happen. Miniatures are also used when something needs to be blown up or crushed by a monster's foot. It is much less expensive to stamp out a toy city than a real city. It is also much easier to clean up!

Miniatures are also used to make something else in the movie look bigger. For instance, in the original King Kong movie, the "giant ape" was really six ape dolls. Each was only eighteen inches high. In the famous scene where Kong climbs the Empire State Building, a miniature replica of the building was built for the set. Each viewer of the film knew that in those days, the Empire State Building was the world's tallest building. When someone saw Kong hanging on the side of it, he looked huge. But Kong was really only hanging from a little model.

Some of the most successful movies of all time have used miniatures to create an image of something that doesn't exist. One of the *Star Wars* movies used miniatures to create a variety of space vehicles. Smith and Blackton had created battle scenes using photos and sticks. The *Star Wars* movie created battles in outer space using miniatures.

To create one miniature, the special effects crew got every ship model possible. They glued pieces of the models to a board. Other parts were added to make it look like a huge spaceship. Then a camera was put in the back of a pick-up truck. As the truck drove by the models, the camera rolled as explosions and sparks were set off on the model. Those shots were used in a big battle scene.

One of the earliest tricks in movie making was the use of *mattes* (mats). A matte is a piece of cardboard or other material. The matte is placed in front of the camera lens. It has a piece cut out of it in a certain shape. This way, all the action in that scene gets filmed through the cutout.

Later, another matte is used to film a background. This matte is the reverse of the first. The area that was blocked in the first matte is now exposed. The two films are then put together, one on top of the other. Though the actors were filmed in a studio, it can look as if the action happened someplace else.

Another special effect is used to make an actor or object appear to be in a location. It is called *blue screen* (or *green screen*) photography. You can see a good example of this every time you watch a local weather report on TV. It looks as if the weather forecasters are standing in front of a weather map, waving their hands over it or pointing to a spot on it. In fact, what you are really seeing are two combined images.

The weather reporters are being shot by the TV camera against a blue background. The camera has a filter on it. It filters out the blue light, so we can't see it. Another camera is focusing on a slide of the weather map. The image of the weather reporters is superimposed, or put on top of, the weather map.

When the two images are combined, it looks as if the reporters are standing in front of a map. In reality, the reporters are pointing at the blue screen behind them. But they are looking at a TV screen that shows the map. Because it is right over the camera, it looks as if they are looking at the camera. They see where they should point.

The same technique is used in film. An actor or object is filmed against a blue or green screen in a film studio. Later, that film gets put together with a film of a location. It makes it look as if the actor has been filmed at that loation.

We have already talked about using a matte. But what happens when you want something to move across a scene? Then you create what is called a *traveling matte.*

In one film, the director was faced with the challenge of showing part of a famous building falling to the city street below. His crew built an eighteen-foot tall model of the top of this building. The model was hoisted into the air by a crane. It was filmed against a green screen when they dropped it. Then the film was developed and changed to show the shape of the building in black. If you saw only that film, you'd see a black shape falling and crashing.

The next step was to film the action of crowds
on the street running away. But the action was
not shot through a cardboard matte. Instead, the
action was shot through that piece of film with
the tower in it. It became a moving matte. If you
showed only that piece of film, you'd see a hole in
the action in the shape of the falling tower. Put
the two films together, and you see the shattered
tower crashing to the ground in the midst of
terrified crowds.

Sometimes tricks are used to make something impossible seem to happen on screen. Sometimes tricks are used to keep people safe. Suppose the script calls for a family to be running away from a burning building. But you don't really want to burn the building. How can you make it safe to shoot that piece of film, but make it look as if the actors are in danger?

One simple way to make it look as if the actors are in danger is to use a long lens on the camera. The long lens, called a *telephoto lens*, can make two things that are far apart look close together. It does that by keeping both items in focus. If you shoot the film with the family running toward the lens, and the fire between the family and the building, then the family is safe. It also makes the building seem to be on fire. If you shot the same scene from the side, you would see a safe distance between the fire and the family.

Many of today's movies use computer-generated images, or CGIs. Computer-generated images can create very believable effects. In this case, the effect still can deceive the eye of the viewer. But it creates images that are often as realistic as real-life actors.

Computer-generated images now solve problems that used to be solved by miniatures or mattes. If a filmmaker can imagine something, a computer operator can probably create it.

Computer effects can be used to create characters on screen. Films have used CGIs to create dinosaurs that look lifelike. They have also been used to make it look as if animals are talking. Some people worry that CGI effects are getting so good that someday actors won't even be needed anymore. That is unlikely—but not entirely impossible!

How is a CGI "actor" created? An actor's body is covered with a grid of straight black lines. Then the actor is filmed, and his movements are scanned by laser to get information about how the actor moves. As the actor moves, the lines bend and move. That information is used by the computer to create a model that looks like a wire frame. Then layers of computer-generated "skin" are put on the wire frame, to create whatever look the director wants. When it is put into motion, the movements are lifelike because they were made by an actor.

Another way computers are used is in *animatronics*. Animatronics is the use of miniature computers, robotics, and make-up to create a realistic creature. Animatronics creates a high-tech puppet. It is something like a cross between a robot and a radio-controlled toy car. Sometimes these creatures are programmed to make certain movements on their own. Sometimes they are controlled by a crew member who tells them what to do.

Stop-motion photography is another common technique. Film is literally moving pictures. A high-speed shutter exposes film at twenty-four pictures per second. In stop-motion photography, a miniature or model is used. A few frames are shot. Then the model is moved a tiny bit. A few more frames are shot. The model is moved again. It is a very slow process. But it can make models have realistic movements.

The original King Kong used stop-motion to make the eighteen-inch gorilla dolls look like a giant ape. Each movement was recorded on film, to make it look as if the ape were climbing.

Today, stop motion is used for "claymation" films. Clay models are put in miniature sets and moved, bit by bit, to make the clay figures' movements look realistic. In the early days of TV, this trick was used for children's programs. Today, you can see the same trick used in programs that entertain children and their parents, and in advertisements as well. Claymation can be very eye-catching.

Movies have come a long way from the early days. Some of the tricks in use today would have seemed impossible in the first days of film. Yet some of the tricks that the early films used are still entertaining audiences today.

As long as filmmakers and script writers have a vision, people will find ways to bring that vision to the screen.

THE END

THE END